To Marissa:
I love designing this life with you.

To Megan:
without you I would not be here.

To my fellow overcomers:
you are no longer alone.

DESIGN YOUR LIFE
Pursuing the Life You Want Without Losing Who You Are
By Carter Reign

1. BODY, MIND & SPIRIT / Inspiration & Personal Growth
2. BUSINESS & ECONOMICS / Entrepreneurship
3. SELF-HELP / Personal Growth / Success

First paperback edition March 2023

Book and cover design by Carter Reign

ISBN 979-8-9879-0080-2 (paperback)
ISBN 979-8-9879-0081-9 (ebook)

www.CarterReign.com

DESIGN YOUR LIFE

Pursuing the Life You Want
Without Losing Who You Are

CARTER REIGN

CONTENTS

INTRO

Does Anyone Really Know?

One of the first books I read when I struck out on my own was *The Wealthy Freelancer*. This book is not new. I had to buy it from the used section on Amazon. It has some really great methods on how to drum up business on day one. However, most of the concepts in it have been vastly improved upon by more recent works. That doesn't make it worthless, it just makes it worth less.

Every book including the one you're holding now has a window into a version of reality. Once you've read a few hundred like I have you can stand back and start to get lost in the sea of contradictions.

The Butterfly Effect and *Atomic Habits* say that you need to make small changes for a big impact.

The 4 Hour Work Week and *Start With Why* say that if you get one thing right, everything else will more or less fall into place.

Grit says that you need to persevere no matter what, but *Daring Greatly* says maybe it's OK to quit.

You Are A Badass clearly contradicts *Humble Strength*.

Malcolm Gladwell says I need 10,000 hours to be an expert, but *Range* suggests that a more diverse experience is more impactful than specializing.

How are we supposed to know who we should be? What tip, trick, or hack, is going to get us that much further ahead? How can we make sure we are the cog that isn't replaced?

Honestly - you can't. That's why you must do the thing that is uniquely yours. Sure, read the books, listen to the experts, and learn from the mistakes that others have made. Then go out and do the work. Don't wait until it's perfect. Don't wait to hit send because of what they'll think. Don't hold back on doing what you were born to do just because you think someone beat you to it.

Go. Be. Live.

How This Book Works

Every action has an equal and opposite reaction.

Many folks have been scared into inaction because of this phrase. However, I'd like to suggest we use it as the starting point for our investigation into the human condition. Perhaps some of the worst realities in our world today can be traced back to something unique inside each and every one of us. Perhaps if we begin to shift what we can in our own world, the rest of humanity will benefit.

This book explores 6 key streams or topics. Here are their loose definitions:

Religion: The systems humanity has developed to make sense of the things we don't understand. The topic of religion encompasses prayer, worship, divinity, power, the spiritual realm, and a whole lot of other activities we might not be able to name. In this book we'll explore the tenants of more common religious sects such as Christianity, Buddhism, and Islam.

Family: Those related to us by blood or bond that we consider our own. Sometimes this means the traditional "family" unit. Other times it means those that have a significant impact on the decisions we make. Father figures, adopted siblings, those that are "like a child" to you can all constitute a family

Trauma: Anything that extends our experience beyond what we can process in the moment. Trauma comes in many forms, but it is an inescapable part of the human experience. To ignore its role in shaping our reality is to blindly react to life as it happens instead of responding to it like the opportunity that it is.

Work: The activities we perform to exchange services, labor, commodities, time, and money. Vocation, career, role, etc. There are many ways to view work. For the purposes of this book we will explore the activities that are loosely known as a job and have to do directly with how we make money.

Identity: The definition of who we really are. We will spend a lot of time on our identity in this book. We'll explore both the external reality of identity and the internal makeup of us. On the surface, it looks a lot like a personality, but underneath it's something much more complex.

Binary: Black vs. white, odd vs. even, winning vs. losing, us vs. them. The world exists in a constant expansion of edges and we are dots in the gray between those edges. This tension helps to keep us grounded and develop the above concepts, but it also drives us to expand the edges and shift our place in the world.

When these 6 streams are out of alignment, these are the consequences:

Religion → Death

Without religious systems our spiritual experiences delve into chaos. Chaos leads us to go mad and eventually the lack of direction leads to death or infinite suffering.

Family → Orphans

If we fail to have a group that we bond with, we develop the worldview of an orphan. We only look out for ourselves, disconnect from reality, and lose the opportunity to make an impact in the world.

Trauma → Mental Health Crisis

The real impact of trauma isn't the moment it occurs - it is the years we live with its impact on our life afterwards. Without addressing and healing traumas, our mind tries to make sense of something nonsensical. It will eventually either drive us mad or into coping mechanisms that are dangerous to us and society.

Work → Resource Shortages

We need humans, intelligence, and emotion to live in the world. However, those entities also need resources to keep living. Work is the system by which we move those resources. Without work, we have no means of exchange and we end up in destitution.

Identity → Suicide

While the issue of suicide is monumentally complex, there is a fundamental element of identity crisis within most instances. If we lose who we are, we disconnect from who we could be. If there's no reason to become, then why should we continue as we are? Eventually the misappropriation of labels will push humanity into the void.

Binary Thinking → Civil Wars

When we experience polarity, we naturally assume we aren't at the edge of it. In chasing the edges we often abandon where we are and begin to distinguish ourselves from others by the deadly act of comparison. This action inevitably leads to fear ruling our society rather than freedom and love. When fear is present, anger and destruction aren't far behind.

This is by no means an exhaustive list, but it provides a solid framework by which we can explore how we got to where we are and how to get to where we want to be.

Throughout this book you'll explore deeper meanings and realities that exist in the above streams, but you'll also be given opportunities along the way to make edits in your reality. There will be guided exercises and journal prompts that will help to expand your thinking and options around your story.

Take your time with this book. Feel free to check the table of contents and start with whichever stream suits you best right now. However, when you pick a stream - follow it to the delta.

Be open to the ways you have always wanted to change your path. With this book as your guide - you just might.

One last thing before you dive in. I am a human. I have limitations, just like everyone else. However, I give the knowledge I have collected freely in hopes that we can move the needle just a little bit. If you want to add to this work, please contact me at book@CarterReign.com.

Abundantly,

Carter

I. THE BINARY

Civil Wars And Gender

*"Every act of war is a mere disagreement
that has gone too far."*
- Unknown

From a young age we are taught right and
wrong. Good and bad. We learn that certain
behaviors are praised and others are frowned
upon. In some ways life is merely a journey to
find our middle. Teenagers are the epitome of
this reality. Always riding the lines and pushing
the limits. Their limit-pushing, however, doesn't
usually last. By the time their prefrontal cortex
develops in their 20s they use their experiences
of the edges to define where they will land.

For me, edge-finding was a journey I traversed on behalf of my gender identity and sexual orientation. I know, I know, I'm sure you thought this book was gonna start on a lighter note.

In my mid-20s I was engaged to a man. I identified at that time as my gender assigned at birth - female. I had spent a lifetime trying to adjust my perspective to find peace with my place on the gender spectrum and hetero-normative lifestyle I'd seen portrayed as the "best way" growing up in an evangelical bubble.

My engagement to this particular man followed a few years of systematic dating I had enacted to try and find anyone that I didn't intimidate and could possibly stand to have in my home. Basically I would line up 3-5 dates every Sunday afternoon and cycle through the eligible bachelors on Coffee Meets Bagel. Looking back I'd say I was staffing the position of husband instead of searching for someone I could create a life with.

I'd been fairly successful professionally despite being in a cult with zero financial support through my early 20s. With a salary of under $40k a year I had bought a home, a car, and two dogs within 2 years of being penniless and homeless. I was living a life I was proud of and had done it all on my lonesome. The last thing I wanted was a "man coming in and trying to prove he was better than me". (Ew, did that just come out of me?)

So what did I do? I went for "we get along". As an INTJ on the Myers Briggs Type Indicator I decided my best odds would be with someone exactly the same as me. Good news - we got along, we made each other laugh, and I didn't hate being around him. The problem? I was bored out of my mind. There were no sparks.

About 3 months before the wedding we called it off and I went on to marry someone that inspired me and gave me all the sparks.

A few years into my relationship with my wife I started to question my gender identity a lot more. If you've ever experienced this, you can probably relate to the countless hours and volumes of inner dialogue I went through trying to find my "spot" on the gender line. I was stuck in the idea that gender was either F, M, or X, and none of those really felt authentic to me.

Thankfully I had Megan. She is one of the wisest and kindest humans I have ever known and I literally owe her my life. Lucky me - we are still friends to this day and even live in the same town. On one of our regular lunch dates I expressed a discontentment with my identity of being female. The question was along the lines of "I don't feel like a woman. Does that make me a man?" and her response will be part of my story forever...

"Maybe the problem you're having isn't about the either/or of male/female. Maybe the problem is in the middle."

To this day I'll swear she had the guru beard and was sitting atop a hill of enlightenment at that moment. Thanks to Megan, I accepted that gender, like most human identifiers, is a spectrum, and I was able to embrace my truest self, so my business took off.

You see, when we think linearly, we assume there is a tipping point. If I'm thinking too liberal, does that make me a democrat? If I like pastels, does that make me a soft person? If I like tofu, am I vegan?

How did I disassemble my messy middle? I decided the issue wasn't linear. If there's no 1 and no 5, I can stop worrying whether I am a 2, 3, or 4.

Quit worrying about where you fall on the line and just be where you are.

On the topic of gender specifically - you can rest knowing there have been such iconic hyper-masculine personalities as the Punisher, Terminator, and the King of Sparta. Odds are, they are more masculine than you so you don't need to worry about falling off the edge. The same applies to the feminine side. We have

Oprah, Dolly Parton, and The Disney Princess roster. Don't worry about falling off the edge - just be where you are. There's no scary middle where you switch over - you just get to be you.

What does gender have to do with civil wars?

Most wars started because two people found themselves on opposite sides of a point and forgot they were still on the same line. If we are all on the same line, the points on that line should be for discussion, not for judgment.

I call that point the "scary middle." It is the point on the line where we are afraid we are too close to the other side, or someone else's opinion that fundamentally differs from ours. We quietly (or not so quietly) worry about the implications of "switching" teams or sides. Often, our worry on the topic causes us to run the opposite direction and end up feeling even more inauthentic than we were when we discovered the scary middle.

Here's the deal – we are always shifting and moving along our lines as we gain more knowledge and understanding of ourselves and the world we live in. Therefore the only purpose of knowing where you're at is to measure yourself against another. Sometimes this can help us as we forge friendships and relationships by identifying others that are similar to us. However, if we use the line to deny realities about ourselves, we will be left spinning our wheels and running from our authentic self.

Judgment isn't usually beneficial unless there is an authority structure already in place. Also, judgment isn't a bad thing. It is a way of assessing reality as it stands in a moment. The cases of life are always open.

When is judgment helpful? Well if I am a parent and you have a different parenting style than I do, I may need to assess how our styles differ so I can determine which one will be enacted with my child. Because I have ultimate authority/responsibility over my family I get to decide which style to enact. Odds are it will be a blend of all my experiences of parenting, but in order to respond to a situation I will need to make a judgment for that moment on how I will act toward my child.

How can you impact the world?

If the matter at hand is something you are directly responsible for (i.e. parenting your child) then you need to decide where you stand on the matter. However, when it comes to understanding where others are coming from - you need to park in neutral. Don't compare where you are to where they are. Here are some questions you can use to employ empathy and better understand someone with your opinion in neutral.

- Tell me more about that.

- If you were to take that to an extreme - what would that look like?

- How do you know you're right about that?

- How long have you felt this way about…

- Would you say your opinion is your own or shared by others you trust?

"You can be right or you can have empathy. You can't do both."

- Seth Godin

Visualization Activity

You can take this chapter further by exploring the civil wars in your own life and family.

1. Think about your parents, partner, or sibling.

2. Recall a disagreement you've had in the past. Recall it to the point where you can remember the title of both sides of the argument.

3. Hit pause on the memory. Imagine yourself floating over into the opposing

person's body. All of a sudden you feel all their memories and emotions. You see their whole life through their eyes.

4. Argue their perspective until you feel your being across from you begin to soften with realization.

5. Float back to your side of the table and back into your body.

6. Smile. Tell them you love them and accept them exactly where they are. Squeeze their hand. Mean it.

Discussion Questions

In the spirit of bringing people together, we've provided some discussion questions for this chapter. Remember to "stay in neutral" as you explore the answers. Always lead with curiosity and wonder.

- What if we've never really elected a great president?

- What if Hitler was right on a few points?

- What if there is life out there?

- What if everyone swept their own front porch? Where would I start with mine?

- What if anything is possible? What would I create?

- What if I've been wrong about every point I've ever held?

- What if being right is impossible?

- What would I do if I knew I couldn't fail?

- What if I decided my life is perfect just the way it is?

- What if it isn't us vs. them? What if it's all just us?

II. IDENTITY

Is Identity A Crisis?

On July 16, 2022 the phone number 988 was designated as the national crisis hotline for suicide prevention. Until then the only hotlines I knew about were 911 for medical emergencies and 411 for before there were smartphones when we needed to know something and couldn't wait until we got to the library or home to our dial-up internet connection.

Researchers around the globe are working tirelessly to understand suicide and mental health more intimately. This is a sensitive subject, and I don't presume I have all the answers to why folks decide that ending their life is better than living another day in it.

However, I will be sharing some ideas that you can implement that I am confident could shift the realities we are facing so 988 may become the new 411. Unnecessary, because we've found a better way.

For several years I was on a team that performed skits for youth around the globe. One of our skits was all about labels. We'd start with an average teen on center stage (usually we used one of our team members so as not to re-traumatize any of the audience participants). We'd have various individuals walk up to them and make a critical statement like "I can't believe you didn't pass that test, it was so easy." and then place a label with the word "DUMB" made of duct tape to the central figure. It was a fairly elementary concept with shockingly deep truths of the permanence of labels and their lasting effects on our lives.

Our whole life we have been collecting labels. Sometimes we wear them proudly and call them our personality. Other times we wear them internally and call them our identity. The problem is that the labels affect us the most and yet are a direct result of our encounters with others. Oftentimes the labels that most clearly define us were stuck to us before we even knew our own name. Expectations from parents, categories defined by society, and dreams of those that couldn't or didn't do themselves. All placed on us and we are expected to just take it.

I say no.

In a perfect world, we would be made of Teflon or respond like my grandma used to say "Be the duck. Those comments are just water."

Unfortunately, the reality of the labels is that most of them do stick and it is our responsibility to remove them before they impact our legacy.

Unlearning Our Labels

Your first option to remove the labels is to go through them one by one and start to peel them off. If you're reading this book the odds are high that you've already tried that and it has either failed or is too painful for you to continue. A lot of individuals have found traditional therapy to be a great Goo-Gone for those pesky labels, but some persist regardless of how many hours we spend on the proverbial couch.

Another option you have is to try and put words to it. Countless personality profiling techniques have been developed to this end. Everything from the more formal MBTI, Enneagram, DISC, Strengthsfinder, etc. all the way to *Buzzfeed's* "Which Disney Princess Are You?" or *Cosmopolitan's* "Find your bedroom superhero type". No matter how much these profiles make you feel seen and understood - they won't ever really have the full picture.

The last option and my personal preference is to design your reality from within. Most of this starts with one really important question:

Who are you, really?

Most people want to quickly respond to this with a bunch of labels. I am a dad. I am a programmer. I am a problem solver.

Resist. The. Urge.

Who you are, really, is so much more than words will be able to describe. Who you are, really, is something sacred. Who you are, really, is paramount to your existence as a member of this wild world. I like to call it your energetic signature.

The Energetic Signature

The Energetic Signature provides a starting point for the ways you will impact the world. It is a unique blend of characteristics that sum up an individual's personality, skills, values, and beliefs. It is a fundamental component of our identity, which influences how we perceive and interact with the world around us. When properly integrated, it is the founding piece you use to design a full and abundant life. This signature defines the core essence of who we are and what we stand for, and it shapes our actions, behaviors, and decision-making processes. When we live in alignment with our Energetic Signature, we feel more authentic and fulfilled. By understanding our Energetic Signature, we can harness our strengths, overcome challenges, and live a more purposeful and powerful life.

Journal Activity

Use the following journal prompts to openly explore pieces of who you are.

What is something you are proud of?

What is a dream you have that you have never told anyone?

If you had a magic wand - what would change about the world?

Go back to being a child in your mind. What textures did you like? What was your favorite color? Describe the desire you felt surrounding yourself with things that met that criteria.

What are traits others consistently recognize in you (positive and negative)?

What do you already know about your personality?

Imagine an army is being assembled to fight an intergalactic being. You don't know exactly what it will be, but you have been told you'll need everyone on earth to battle it. The intake agent asks you for your superpower. It's something no one else on earth can do as well as you. It's probably a combination of hard and soft skills. Be lengthy and be specific.

How would you define your superpower or your *Energetic Signature*?

What Makes You Tick?

"Sometimes the smallest things take up the most room in your heart."

— **Winnie the Pooh**

Values

We all have them. They are the silent rules that guide our lives, our true North, our "because" in life. Most of our values are installed during childhood by influences like our parents and teachers. Some of our values are adopted as we navigate through complex or difficult situations. No matter where you got them, everyone has values. They help us make decisions based on what is important to us. The world comes with a whole lotta roads, but not a lot of roadmaps. Values keep us going even when we don't know where we are.

To explore your values and learn more about how they impacted you, first you'll need to identify them. Scan this list and jot down any that stand out to you. If you were to rate each value between 1 (not important) and 5 (very important) you'll only jot down the ones that are a 5. To help avoid overwhelm, limit yourself to 10 maximum values at once. If you have 10 written down and find one that needs to go on the list, you must remove one before you add it. Stick to your values, and you can be proud of how you show up in any situation.

Acceptance	Calm
Accomplishment	Candor
Accountability	Capable
Accuracy	Careful
Achievement	Certainty
Adaptability	Challenge
Alertness	Charity
Altruism	Cleanliness
Ambition	Clear
Amusement	Clever
Assertiveness	Comfort
Attentive	Commitment
Awareness	Common sense
Balance	Communication
Beauty	Community
Boldness	Compassion
Bravery	Competence
Brilliance	Concentration

Confidence	Development
Connection	Devotion
Consciousness	Dignity
Consistency	Discipline
Contentment	Discovery
Contribution	Drive
Control	Effectiveness
Conviction	Efficiency
Cooperation	Empathy
Courage	Empower
Courtesy	Endurance
Creation	Energy
Creativity	Enjoyment
Credibility	Enthusiasm
Curiosity	Equality
Decisive	Ethical
Decisiveness	Excellence
Dedication	Experience
Dependability	Exploration
Determination	Expressive

Fairness

Family

Famous

Fearless

Feelings

Ferocious

Fidelity

Focus

Foresight

Fortitude

Freedom

Friendship

Fun

Generosity

Genius

Giving

Goodness

Grace

Gratitude

Greatness

Growth

Happiness

Hard work

Harmony

Health

Honesty

Honor

Hope

Humility

Humor

Imagination

Improvement

Independence

Individuality

Innovation

Inquisitive

Insightful

Inspiring

Integrity

Intelligence

Intensity	Order
Intuitive	Organization
Joy	Originality
Justice	Passion
Kindness	Patience
Knowledge	Peace
Lawful	Performance
Leadership	Persistence
Learning	Playfulness
Liberty	Poise
Logic	Potential
Love	Power
Loyalty	Present
Mastery	Productivity
Maturity	Professionalism
Meaning	Prosperity
Moderation	Purpose
Motivation	Quality
Openness	Realistic
Optimism	Reason

Recognition	Simplicity
Recreation	Sincerity
Reflective	Skill
Respect	Skillfulness
Responsibility	Smart
Restraint	Solitude
Results-oriented	Spirit
Reverence	Spirituality
Rigor	Spontaneous
Risk	Stability
Satisfaction	Status
Security	Stewardship
Self-reliance	Strength
Selfless	Structure
Sensitivity	Success
Serenity	Support
Service	Surprise
Sharing	Sustainability
Significance	Talent
Silence	Teamwork

Temperance

Thankful

Thorough

Thoughtful

Timeliness

Tolerance

Toughness

Traditional

Tranquility

Transparency

Trust

Trustworthy

Truth

Understanding

Uniqueness

Unity

Valor

Victory

Vigor

Vision

Vitality

Wealth

Welcoming

Winning

Wisdom

Wonder

Beliefs

Values and beliefs are both important aspects of an individual's worldview, but they differ in their nature and scope. Values are the guiding principles or standards that individuals use to judge what is important or desirable in life, such as the ones listed in the last section. These values are deeply held and shape an individual's behavior and decision-making processes. Beliefs, on the other hand, are specific ideas or convictions that individuals hold to be true, such as religious or political beliefs. Beliefs may be influenced by personal experience, cultural or societal norms, or other factors, and can vary widely among individuals. While values and beliefs are related, they are distinct concepts that play different roles in shaping an individual's worldview.

You may agree with them and you may not, but here are a few beliefs held by a surprising number of people:

- Belief in a higher power or deity: Many people believe in the existence of an otherworldly being that governs the universe and influences human affairs.

- Belief in the afterlife: This can look like many things, including heaven, hell, reincarnation, or spiritual realms.

- Belief in the power of positive thinking: This refers to manifestation and visualization helping people achieve their goals and improve their lives.

- Belief in the importance of family: Many people believe that family is the most important social unit and that maintaining strong familial relationships is crucial for personal happiness and well-being. This can be both your biological and your chosen family.

- Belief in the value of hard work: Effort and perseverance are necessary for success, and people who work hard are more deserving of success than those who do not.

- Belief in the importance of community: Humans are social creatures and building strong communities is essential for personal happiness and well-being.

- Belief in the power of love: Love is the most powerful force in the universe, and it can conquer hate, fear, and even death.

I challenge you to spend some time exploring your own beliefs about life and your existence. These beliefs are a key piece of why you are the way you are today. If you want to create a new life for yourself, you may need to change your beliefs.

When you discover a belief you'd like to shift, I recommend the Socratic method. Here are a list of questions you can ask yourself to begin to reshape your beliefs:

1. What is the belief that you want to question?

2. What is the evidence for this being true?

3. What is the evidence against this being true?

4. How could you be misinterpreting the evidence?

5. What assumptions are you making?

6. Could others have a different interpretation or perspective?

7. What could some of those be?

8. Are you examining ALL the evidence or just that which supports your belief?

9. Could this belief be an exaggeration of the truth?

10. The more that you think about the evidence and differing perspectives, is this belief the truth?

11. Is this belief just a habit you have gotten into or does the evidence support it?

12. Did this belief originate from someone else?

13. Are they a reliable source of fact?

14. Does this belief serve you in ALL situations in your life?

15. Does this belief help or restrict you in life?

16. What do you think about this belief now? Give details...

What do you need?

Whew. That was a lot of soul searching. Hopefully by now you know enough about yourself to really make an impact on how you move through the world. Ideally, you have discovered your Energetic Signature, understood more about how your experiences have shaped your current reality, examined and altered your beliefs about yourself, and explored how your values can align to help propel you into the life of your dreams. Now let's explore the final piece of the puzzle that is you.

Needs

As soon as you identify something in your life as a "need" and not a "want," your whole brain and the energy around and in you goes to work to acquire that thing.If you need food on a road trip, your eyes start to search for the next exit. If you need sleep, your brain starts to shut the processes down that are used to keep you awake. If you need time, you make it.

In 1943, a guy named Abraham Maslow wrote a paper titled "A Theory of Human Motivation". In this paper he began to explore what motivates people to do the things we do. Since then, we have continued to build on the idea with ever increasing curiosity and refer to it as Maslow's Hierarchy of Needs.

Maslow's Hierarchy of Needs is a psychological theory that proposes that humans have a set of needs that must be met in a specific order to achieve self-actualization, or the realization of one's full potential. Maslow identified five categories of needs, arranged in a pyramid-shaped hierarchy, with the most basic physiological needs at the bottom and the highest level of self-actualization at the top. The five categories of needs are:

1. Physiological Needs: These are the most basic human needs, including food, water, air, shelter, and sleep. Without meeting these needs, a person cannot survive.

2. Safety Needs: Once physiological needs are met, the next level of needs includes safety and security, such as a stable living environment, job security, and personal safety.

3. Love and Belonging Needs: Once a person's physiological and safety needs are met, they seek out social connections and relationships with

others, including love, friendship, and a sense of belonging.

4. Esteem Needs: The fourth level of needs includes self-esteem and the desire for respect and recognition from others. This includes both internal and external esteem, such as self-confidence and the respect of others.

5. Self-Actualization Needs: The highest level of needs in Maslow's Hierarchy is self-actualization, which is the realization of one's full potential and the pursuit of personal growth, creativity, and fulfillment.

Maslow's theory suggests that people must meet each lower level of needs before they can move on to the next level. Once basic physiological needs are met, people seek out safety and security, then love and belonging, followed by esteem, and finally self-actualization. The theory has been influential in the fields of psychology, education, and business management.　　However, Maslow also recognized that individuals may move up and down the hierarchy depending on life circumstances and individual experiences.　If these needs aren't met, we behave like hangry children who need a snack before they can be reasoned with. When we are children, we rely on others to get our needs met, but we still take personal responsibility to express those needs. As we get older, our needs become more complex. We begin to need our values and beliefs to be supported and actualized. We need to be heard by our peers and affect change in our communities. Establishing which needs are most imperative is another step on the path to self-fulfillment.

Activity

Take each of the levels of the pyramid and pick only one need to measure on a regular basis. Pick ones that you notice are often existing unfulfilled. For instance, if you live with your parents, let's assume shelter isn't your top physical need. It may be rest or good food.

Now I want you to envision your life with a dashboard. You can customize it and give it cool lights and colors if you want, but you need to have a way to see how full each need is. Think of the needs like buckets and make sure these 5 needs are met. Check your dashboard often and make sure no buckets are empty.

The fun part comes by getting creative with how we get our needs met. One of my most important needs is physical touch. During a time in my life when I wasn't dating and wasn't being touched a lot, I had to get creative. I went out to eat at crowded places, hung out with my friends' kids, and got a pet. Before my notion of the needs buckets, I might have kept searching or gotten back into the dating pool too quickly, but because I was able to recognize this unmet need and then intentionally fill the "bucket," I knew I'd be OK. Re-establishing how we fill our buckets is extra necessary when we go through big life changes —like a new town, breakups, or the death of a loved one.

Most of our lives are lived on auto-pilot with our needs buckets being filled and emptied on a regular basis. If you can not only live life, but understand how these processes work inside yourself, you will be in a much more powerful position to affect the outcome of circumstances that are beyond your control.

The Self Actualization Cycle

Life is one big system. We are all ultimately connected to a source of life that provides for our needs. We are responsible for how we use those resources to create our reality. It goes something like this:

Source > Resources > Energetic Signature > Values > Beliefs > Actions > Reality

We are given resources by a source that desires us to live. As we utilize those resources to bring about growth and freedom we filter our actions through our values and beliefs until our actions create our reality.

So let's go back to the 988 topic. Where does suicide happen? Where do we need to make a change to prevent it? Odds are that it happens at the end, but the changes need to be made in every area of a person's life if we are going to affect the outcome. Most people are just editing actions without getting down to the real root causes. Start to change the tide of reality by understanding who you are as a whole being, not just the labels you have collected by living.

III. WORK

Working To Live

"Opportunity is missed by most people because it is dressed in overalls and looks like work."

- *Thomas Edison*

Work. It's a common enough word. Yet how we interpret it varies wildly from person to person and oftentimes from moment to moment.

From mowing lawns on Saturday mornings to being overworked and underpaid in the corporate world, at one point or another, most everyone has had a job.

When I began my career as an entrepreneur I had to recategorize a large portion of my activities. Reading a nonfiction book was no longer killing time, it was work. For me work isn't a negative thing or a burden. Work is simply a label I place on activities that have financial resources flowing with them.

Different cultures around the world highlight the true differences in how we view work and can show us the outcome that certain worldviews on work can impact every area of life. In some countries napping is expected at work. Some cultures shame those that work less than 80 hours. Some cultures have children working instead of enjoying childhood. Some cultures have even tried to abandon the concept of work altogether.

For the purposes of this book, we'll limit our exploration of the modern work environment to the United States.

As everyone knows, COVID-19 did a number on the general work experience. The most obvious change was, of course, mass layoffs. The second is remote working, everyone's favorite excuse to wear PJs to work. Despite these changes, there are still remnants of the corporate culture that aren't long for this world. Gen-Z is doing a great job of shaking things up by throwing out the typical and traditional corporate "rules," but we still have a ways to go.

Most of the world is still participating in work that looks a lot like a machine. Many smaller cogs that are working to move the machine forward and achieve a result that no one cog could do alone. Of course the concern with being a cog in someone else's machine is that at some point you will be replaced. We've seen this reality even more recently with the evolution of artificial intelligence. For a while we thought purely creative jobs would be safe, but even those have been impacted by the latest generation of AI art generators.

Your only real defense against being replaced is to create a work option for yourself that is uniquely yours and tied to your Energetic Signature. No one can take that from you.

Of course, I'm biased and hope that many people will choose entrepreneurship as a means of creating their own unique work in the world, but that's not for everyone. Even if you are in a more corporate environment, you can still advocate for your position to align with who you are. Take the flow diagram from the last chapter, but this time apply it to your work. Don't just edit your actions or complain about work - edit the way your work flows through your life.

Journal Activity

What resources are available to you?

With those resources in your hands, what skills will you have?

Do you need to uplevel any of those skills or talents to align your work with your own level of value you need to uphold in your work?

If you approach your tasks with your entire emotional and logical bank of knowledge - how would that change the way you showed up?

Are you advocating for your needs?

How could you refine your communication style or requests to better align them with positive outcomes?

Who do you believe you can serve and uplift naturally without any real strain on your life system or self?

What priceless value do you bring to your work?

Is your current role a place that appropriately validates your indisputable value?

How can you better communicate the value of your work?

Are you willing to make a change if it means you get to do more work aligned with your Energetic Signature?

Don't Quit Your Day Job

When I am working with a client, 9 times out of 10 they are able to make a minor change in their work and they encounter a staggering improvement in their performance. It's more likely to be a burr in the saddle than a stray bullet that derails the journey of a thousand miles.

Sure, you might need to change jobs or start a company. But what if you don't? Baby with the bathwater and all that...

Good Enough

There are a handful of "rules" that the self-help community has developed to help us achieve a greater sense of balance in our lives. My version of the 80/20 rule goes something like this...

80% of your results come from 20% of your effort. Also, C's get degrees and 80% will usually be "good enough".

Another way of putting this might be "work smarter, not harder".

Perhaps you've always been an overachiever or perfectionist. When you do something, you do it well. However, you realize that there's too much you'd like to do in this life and frankly not enough time or resources to do it all. This is the permission you've been waiting for to stop giving 100%.

Why not give 100%? Because there are limits to certain areas of life. It is the human prerogative to constantly press against and expand those limits, but let's say for arguments sake that you are limited to 100% that you can give. Now you've got a choice to make: would you rather give 100% to one thing, or get 80% completed results on 5 things? Do you want to be a 100% amazing friend… or be an 80% good parent, 80% successful athlete, 80% solid employee, 80% good sibling, and 80% good friend.

The point is, the amount of improvement you'll see between giving 20% and giving

100% is negligible for the amount of resources it consumes.

Give yourself permission to declare something "good enough". Stop striving to be excellent and the best at everything. Do what you can, then trust the rest of the process.

IV. TRAUMA

Pesky Porches

*"If everyone swept their own front porch
the whole world would be clean."*

*- My Famously Meddlesome
Grandmother*

You're right, I'm sure someone else said that long before my grandmother graced the world with her quips and phrases, but she's the one I heard it from.

As I grew up I realized just how many folks don't sweep their porches, metaphorically speaking. So naturally I had to ask myself why? Why don't people take care of themselves?

Don't we want a clean world? I've come up with a few theories:

1. What porch?

Maybe when these folks were younger the porch was too overwhelming. Or the opposite - their parents kept it nice and clean and never taught them the honest truth about responsibility and accountability. I can say I have met a startling number of people that truly have no idea they have a role to play. My response to that is that everyone has a role and you can only ignore it for so long. Willful ignorance is not a bull I waste my time on. If this is you - you have a porch. Even if it's very small - start taking responsibility.

2. They don't have a broom

Some folks don't have this book. They honestly don't have access to the resources they need to be able to care for themselves in the way you and I can. I don't have an answer for them. My belief is that of the great Albus Dumbledore - help will always come to those that ask. So wherever they are in the world I hope they keep asking. Keep seeking. In my experience when I am willing to seek and to receive the help that is sent my way I always end up with exactly what I need. Most hardware stores have 10 different types of brooms, and most folks have resources to share.

3. It's already clean

Reality is deftly avoided by comparison and "clean" is often a standard somewhat fudged by many porch owners. Welcome to excuse central. "I cleaned it last week", "Mine is cleaner than his", "It's clean enough for now", "Nobody cares when I clean it more than this" and so on. To this I plead with you - improve a little every day. Comparing ourselves to others is not a sustainable way to improve our own habits and ways of life. Learn something. Try something. Improve on what already is. Dream about what could be. Imagine a bigger porch. Make your standards your own and then lift them just a bit. Growing is the only way we can change our reality.

4. "No can do, partner."

Personal responsibility is a fact of my existence. However, I can't assume that it is that way for everyone else. There will always be people that choose to not clean their proverbial porch because they truly believe they can't. If you encounter someone like that - cut them off and make tracks. You are not going to convince them they can by continually showing off your own porch. Commenting on the filth of their own porch won't do much good, either. Eventually they will resent you no matter what you do. People who don't want to change will find every excuse not to, and you'll lose them anyways.

So you want to sweep your porch?

The idea of everyone sweeping their porch alludes to the effectiveness of systems of responsibility. Each person does their unique part and the whole benefits.

66

When I was healing from my trauma, one of the things that kept me going was the thought of all those I could help when I found a way out of the darkness. I decided the quicker I got to the light, the more people I could help. I hit the gas.

For some people they would rather take the long way. Heal each hole in the wall and wait for it to dry, then paint it, then move to the next one. However, I'm not wired like that. I'm a batch guy. I will make time and sink my teeth into any task I see value in. Take this book - I wrote it in 2 days. Granted, I have a lifetime of experiences and years of professional coaching that gave me the knowledge I needed to pull from. However, once I was ready, I just did it. The same was true of my healing journey.

I experienced a high level of trauma in my childhood and early adult years. Because of this, my first therapist felt that I would need a more experienced therapeutic setting than she could provide. With wisdom, she offered to connect me with her mentor. That mentor felt the same. At the end I was passed "up" to more experienced therapists 6 times. However, the one I landed with wasn't actually a therapist. She was a life coach.I was handed papers stating I understood that she had no licensing, but that she did have what I needed. I believed her and signed without hesitation.

During our sessions we worked through problems at a rate that would have most folks weeping for days. I didn't care. I processed what I needed to and moved on to the next thing. This worked until we came to healing "parts". Part therapy saved my life and has had a massive impact on my work as a coach. (For more reading, check out *No Bad Parts* by Richard Schwartz or research Internal Family Systems).

Her approach was to "integrate" these parts one at a time into my current consciousness. This work was tedious and needlessly time-consuming. At one point my patience with the process wore thin and I asked her to integrate all the rest of the parts at once. She was not on board at first and adamantly explained that the process could kill me.

I decided I'd rather die than drag it out any more and postpone my ability to help others at my full capacity. She supported my right to alter my therapeutic experience, and we pushed forward.

BTW - Do not try this unless you have the best facilitator in the world. It was intense.

But we did it.

You're probably not like me. And trust me when I say that is a *very* good thing. However, I hope that you can maybe take a step to get a little uncomfortable. Go a little faster than you have before. Don't spend as much time getting that broom into every crevice of your life. If you push yourself just enough, you can help countless others who are unable to do the work.

Trauma and Range

Thanks to studies and research around mental health taking the front seat in scientific communities over the last few decades we know more than we ever have about the concept. In case you aren't familiar, I'll quickly explain the two important distinctions in trauma.

Important: all trauma and experiences are valid. We do not measure or compare one trauma as more or less than another.

For the purposes of this book we are going to talk about "big T" Trauma. "Little t" trauma happens almost daily in our world. The door closing louder than you thought it would, the dog barking, the water boiling before you have the pasta, or getting a call from someone you haven't heard from in years.

Trauma, both big and little T, happens when something occurs in our reality that expands our consciousness. When we encounter trauma it may surprise us, but it doesn't break us.

We have a range in our consciousness of what is possible at any given moment. If you imagine what could happen in your world on a ruler, little t trauma might bend the ruler a bit or add a mm to the end of the ruler. Big T Trauma snaps it in half or adds another 4 feet to the end of it. The ruler tries to stretch, but it just can't. It breaks.

The reason I say all trauma is valid is that each person is not 12in by default. We have all different capacities for what we can handle in our current reality. The good news is that we can stretch, the bad news is that most stretching happens without our consent and at a rate that often breaks us in today's world.

So what do you do with Trauma?

Accept it

It happened. You cannot go back and change reality. Let go of those that caused it. Unforgiveness is taking a poison pill and hoping the other person will die. All you can do at this point is to reconcile it in your own mind and understand it enough so you can…

Heal from it

Maybe you need a therapist to help you do it, or maybe you need balance. A major byproduct of Trauma is that it puts us out of balance. When we encounter a tragedy we feel tipped in what we expect of the world. Things look a little more bleak than they have before. The fastest way to heal is to rebalance this. Go pet puppies. Go skydiving. Paint for 7 days straight. Do something that brings you unbelievable joy. Rebalance your experience so you can…

Share it

Once we heal from Trauma we have an increased capacity. We can do an unbelievable amount of good with that capacity. We can help others that feel broken in that space. We can extend our capacity to others so they don't break. And we can help hold space for those that need to heal.

Don't let Trauma destroy you. It will help you become who you are meant to be.

How Time Impacts the Mind

You are here, now. It's important to establish that you can only exist at one moment in time at a time. While I'm sure there are folks that are exploring time travel, right now the only way we can go from here into the past or the future is in our minds. However, there are some limitations.

Various studies have explored just how much our brain can store. The current conclusion is that everything is remembered, but not everything can be recollected. Our mind catalogs all the information it collects, and "good" memory usually comes down to how effectively we can navigate that catalog. To expedite this process, the mind has established dominant processing centers to both the past and the future.

Since we do not actually know how we will feel about an encounter in the future, we process it through our logical mind. Perhaps the weather will be off that day or you will get a fancy job proposal the day before or you will lose a loved one. All of those things might affect how you feel about a certain encounter. Therefore, we can establish that we process the future dominantly through our logical mind.

Then there's the past. As life is happening in real-time you can imagine that there is a red "Recording" light on in your mind. However, in real-time there is an enormous amount of data being processed. The logical facts are rather small bites of information. For example, the carpet was red, the sun was visible, it was 2:53, and so on. However, the emotional data is much more complex and volumus.

I felt like he wasn't really listening to me…

my mind felt a little foggy…

the sound was louder than usual…

I felt like the conversation would never end...

And so on.

When we recall that memory for any reason, odds are the only data we will be able to bring up is the emotional data. We will likely present it as fact, but odds are the facts are just the truth about how we felt.

"He yelled at me until my head hurt!"

If we operate under the assumption that all past data is emotional and all future data is logical, we can begin to understand why it is important to integrate it all.

We need the emotional data from the past and the logical data of the future to fully stand in our power today and decide how we will navigate this life. It is paramount that we not spend too much time either the past or the future as the only place we really have the power to make edits in our story is now.

You Have Staff

"I don't get it. Everyone my whole life has told me I was meant for greatness. People are constantly impressed by me, but they have to be mistaken. I see myself in the mirror every day and – let me tell you – it's not that impressive. What do they see that I don't?"

I had this conversation with my brother when he was at a breaking point after life had dealt him more than one bad hand. He needed a new way to view himself and his abilities. Due to some misunderstandings and miscommunications, my family and I had been nearly estranged for about 10 years. This conversation with my brother was the beginning of what would be our new relationship and I knew the stakes were high.

I want to walk you through the exercise just like I did for him. Hopefully, at the end, you will exclaim the same thing:

"I have staff!"

Visualization Activity

Everything we are about to work through is going to happen in your mind. Just like any other mindset shift, prepare to do the work by deciding the outcome you are hoping for and getting to a calm and quiet place to do the work.

Take a few deep breaths and get your creative juices flowing. Think of yourself as a master designer. We need to make a room.

This room will hereafter be referred to as your boardroom. This is the place where you will assemble different pieces of your subconscious to work through difficult life situations.

Begin to assemble the details of the room. What color are the walls? Are there walls? Tables? Bean bag chairs? Swings? A glass whiteboard? Fidget toys? What is the theme? Where do you sit?

This process can take a few minutes, but it's important to take time to observe the details as they will be the backdrop for many future breakthroughs.

When you're good and the space is ready - think of an issue you'd like to solve, the more specific the instance the better. Give the situation a title. This can be things like "The way I feel in the mornings", "When I yell at my kids" or "My sister called me lazy yesterday".

Put the title up on whatever screen you designed for the boardroom. If you didn't include one in the initial plan, that's fine. You can install one in a second just by making it so. Whether it's a big screen TV or a holographic display like Iron Man - just make sure it's up there in big readable letters.

As soon as the title is up, you can invite all the relevant parties into the boardroom. Typically they appear all at once, but some may be trickling in as you sort through the situation.

Take roll by eye contact. Start to scan around the boardroom and notice who is there. You may have parts like Compassion, Questioner,

The Flippant One, Hurt, or Ego. There's no limit to how many parts can be in the room, but I usually can identify 5-8 with about 15-20 in the room for significant discussions. Don't worry too much about identifying every person there, just note the most present ones and then do a scan for the first one that seems out of sorts or agitated.

Invite that part over or go to where it is existing. Take notes on how the part is behaving. Jumping up and down, looking terrified, shaking its head, swinging from the rafters. Notice relevant details on its appearance. Short, bug-eyed, scowling, crying, etc.

Interact with the part with compassion, intention, and wonder. You are the "adult" in this situation, even if the part isn't a child. You have more context and faculties to sort through what's going on and the part is relying on you to guide the conversation. This will be a negotiation with the part so begin wherever you feel is appropriate. The goal is to get the part enrolled in the issue at hand and help it sort out any issues or trauma it has around the topic.

Here is a basic script/flow:

Greeting - Hello, what's your name?

Validation - That's a great name!

Inquiry - What do you have there?

Rapport building - I have something like that, but yours seems better

Profile - What do you do here?

Validation - That's super helpful! I really appreciate that you do that for me.

Focus - When we put [issue] up on the screen you seemed to be upset. Can you tell me why?

Validation - Oh wow, well, I can see how you thought that. But, did you know [full perspective] so [negative thing] won't happen anymore. I can help protect you.

Check in - Are you ok to participate now?

Probing - You seem like you're feeling [emotion], do you know why?

Understanding - Wow, I can see how that would be _____.

Offer - How can I help?

Creativity - What if we did _____ so that [emotion resolved]?

Magic - Poof! There we go, the [belief/perception] has changed.

Check in - How does that feel? Are you ready to rejoin the others?

Option 2 - You're welcome to stay as we discuss this, but you don't have to.

These parts are pieces of your subconscious that are constantly running programs and scripts based on information they have acquired during your lifetime. Many times these parts are forged in times of high emotion and therefore cannot fully process similar scenarios without bringing the same emotion to the table.

It is important that you realize you have unlimited creativity during these interactions. Remember, you know yourself best. Sometimes you'll need to get the part a new tool, sometimes they need help, sometimes they need clothes, sometimes they just want to go for a walk or play with their friends instead of being in the room.

These parts are a part of you (pun intended). The more meetings you host and interactions you have with the parts of yourself the more mastery you will have in your boardroom and the larger the issues you'll be able to handle will become.

As always, if you feel a part is too traumatized or you aren't able to handle it without losing yourself - get help. Look for therapists trained in IFS or a coach that can help you get the parts of yourself in order.

Enjoy the journey of enrolling the help of the different parts of yourself and marvel at how much greater your capacity becomes. It's no longer just you and the conscious knowledge you have at any given moment, it's you PLUS a staff of parts that remember everything you need to solve any issue that comes your way.

You have staff.

V. FAMILY

Reality > Fairytale

Once upon a time, in a faraway kingdom, there was a teenage prince who lived a life of luxury and ease. His father, the king, was a great warrior who fought dragons to protect the kingdom. However, the prince had no interest in the affairs of the kingdom and refused to take on any responsibilities while his father was away.

Despite his father's warnings, the prince continued to spend his days in idleness, wasting away his time on frivolous activities. He failed to understand the gravity of his father's role in protecting the kingdom and the importance of taking up his own responsibilities.

One day, the king went to fight a particularly fierce dragon, and unfortunately, he did not return. The news of the king's demise came as a shock to the prince. The kingdom was thrown into chaos, and the prince was left to face the challenges of ruling a kingdom unprepared.

For the first few years, the prince continued to live in denial, believing that someone else would come to save the kingdom. However, as time went by, he began to realize the extent of his neglect and how much damage had been done to the kingdom.

It was only after much soul-searching that the prince finally came to understand his role in the kingdom. He realized that he had to take responsibility for his actions and that the kingdom's fate was in his hands. He worked hard to restore the kingdom to its former glory, but it was too late.

The kingdom had already fallen into ruin, and it took years of hard work and sacrifice to bring it back to life. The prince learned a valuable lesson about the importance of taking personal ownership, but the lesson could have been much shorter if he'd taken action sooner.

Rulers Rule

You cannot wait another day to take authority over your life.

It is continually surprising to me how many therapists spend 80% of their sessions diving into the past. They are adhering to an antiquated practice that the answers for where we are today will be answered by something long gone.

I am a survivor of sexual abuse. I am a survivor of trafficking. I am a survivor of intimate emotional abuse. I am a survivor of many things others did to try and dim my light. And that's the end of it.

What happened does not define what I am capable of, nor does it limit what I am responsible for.

What happened to you is not your fault, but it is your responsibility. Decide today that the generational patterns will stop with you. Commit to healing yourself just enough to move past it. There is hope on the other side. There is a new way. You are the only one that needs to decide it's OK to move on.

Choose healing. Choose freedom. Choose you.

Blame

"But you don't know my mother."

If I could only count the number of times I've heard an excuse like this one. Sometimes it's what their uncle did, or their dad didn't do, or their mom tried to do, or their sister did and didn't tell anyone.

My preferred response comes from the great philosopher, Rafiki:

> *"It does not matter.*
> *It's in the past."*

However, sometimes it does matter. Sometimes those wounds refuse to heal.

For most issues surrounding family, I recommend traditional talk therapy. It can work wonders to have someone sit across from you and validate that whatever happened, happened to you, and you're not wrong to feel what you feel. If talk therapy is too intense, ask for a practitioner that is well versed in EMDR. This therapeutic technique enables you to revisit memories without triggering trauma responses.

If you've tried the therapy route and are still frustrated when you try to deal with family issues, the next step is boundaries.

Some of my favorite work on boundaries comes from Brené Brown. I highly recommend reading some of her work or listening to her podcasts to learn more about how you can install boundaries in your life.

I do work intimately with clients to create systems of success within their families, but because family situations can vary so wildly, I will not be providing a ton of advice in this book about it. For now I will give these three broad suggestions:

1. **Be clear and concise.** No means no, 5 minutes means 5 minutes, and when you set a boundary you must stick to it. Commit to the boundary before you are in a situation where it can be challenged and then do not negotiate.

2. **Have a wingman.** Children are fundamentally programmed to respond to their family members in certain situations. If you find yourself always leaving family interactions a little foggy and upset –take someone with you. Give them clear instructions and permission to pull you out if the situation gets too dicey. Ask them to advocate for the person you know you are capable of being. Go in with a game plan and then stick to it.

3. **Take a break.** If you always go home for Christmas or have family dinner every Sunday night, maybe you need a break. Give yourself permission to not show up next time. Take a mental health break from family obligations in the same way you might from work. Sometimes if you are outside the family dynamic long enough you'll come back with the knowledge you need to erect boundaries within the walls of your family system.

Journal Activity

How do you define personal responsibility, and what does it mean to you?

Think about a time when you took full responsibility for a situation. How did it make you feel, and what did you learn from the experience?

What are some areas of your life where you struggle with taking responsibility? Why do you think that is, and what steps can you take to address it?

Think about a time when you tried to avoid taking responsibility for something. What was the outcome, and what could you have done differently?

What role does accountability play in personal responsibility, and how do you hold yourself accountable?

What are some ways you can take more ownership of your life, both in terms of your actions and your mindset?

What does it mean to be responsible for your own happiness, and how can you cultivate a sense of personal fulfillment?

What are some habits or practices you can develop to help you become more responsible and accountable in your daily life?

VI. RELIGION

Systems And Frameworks

What if? What if this isn't the first time we've had a civilization at the unfathomable edge of possibility. Several archaeologists have unearthed evidence that supports highly sophisticated and technologically advanced civilizations from millions of years ago. But that's another book.

What if Jesus was a guru? What if religion is simply a framework that humans have used for the past few thousand years to explain things they could not comprehend? Topics like healing feels supernatural, so let's attribute the effects to a deity. I thought long and hard about something I wanted, and it came true. Let's call it praying. Emotion feels like it's too big for my frame, so let's bring it outside us, sing really loudly, and call it worship. Commitment feels like I might decide to change my mind, so let's make it scary if I do and save me from myself. Those lights in the sky are always moving, and planetary rotation doesn't exist yet, so I bet they are gods.

Not too long ago we embarked on a new information age. The world wide web emerged and we were able to share knowledge at an unprecedented rate. Record keeping went digital and we didn't have to worry about moving the scrolls in the monsoon season. We accelerated our learning with institutions and created communities where many minds worked together to comprehend mysteries at a whole new level. We enlisted the help of computing power and solved problems faster than we could when they were slowed by the curious human mind. We developed artificial intelligence and gave it just enough data and curiosity to be able to reach the corners of the world we'd been unaware of for as long as we can remember. Now what?

Going Cosmic

We've gone from 1 to 2 to 3 to 4 dimensions.

A quick search led me to a Smithsonian article stating (with a good level of evidence and traditional scientific authority) that there are likely 10 dimensions. However, the search also led to sites claiming 14, 26, and even infinite dimensions. Suffice to say there are significantly more ways of looking at things than we originally thought. We need to accept we are probably more ignorant than we will ever know.

With access to all the knowledge we need to understand what can currently be understood - what do we do now? Humanity craves understanding and exploration. It turns out Star Trek wasn't as crazy as we thought.

Here's my big statement:

Religion was a mechanism by which we understood what had been experienced in this world. What if that framework no longer serves the need to explore beyond what we currently experience?

Unlike the philosophers in ancient Greece, we do not necessarily have the luxury of time. We are exploring and expanding our knowledge at a rate never seen before in this iteration of humanity. We can only sit and debate what to call dark matter for so long before we just have to acknowledge it exists and move on to the next frontier.

What if?

This is my favorite question, and the one I pose to my clients most often. Short and initially harmless, this simple question has the power to pull out your "why," unearth your hesitations, and expose your truest goals and desires. This question usually turns out to be massively uncomfortable, because it also exposes just how much we don't know. It can be as simple as what if I turn left instead of right, or as complex as "What if we didn't worry about what everyone else saw a few thousand years ago?" and throw our preconceived notions to the wind?

What if we rely on more than what we know from our five senses to navigate a world filled with opportunities of expanding our consciousness? Would this open up our concept of reality and help us grow into our fullest potential?

What if we assume that the universe is much larger than what the light rays have carried to our feeble eyes? Would this help us allow space for the unknown to exist and expand the limits to our creativity?

What if we operate on the basis that knowledge exists beyond what we can currently communicate with our words? Would this help us expand our vocabulary to learn all we possibly can?

"What if?" is my favorite question because of its power to unlock. I use this question to get to the root of an issue, the reason behind a trauma, or bring up a realistic view of a situation.

We Hate the Unknown

Nature abhors a vacuum. It is probably one of the most well-known Aristotle idioms (even if you didn't know it was him), and subsequently repeated by many other historically philosophical people until we all agreed it was one that perfectly describes human nature. Overall, we hate the concept of the unknown, and our psyches will automatically fill in any gaps with something we know to be true.

This used to be a basal survival tactic, but since we are no longer running for our lives on a daily basis, it is a strangely limiting belief. Embracing the unknown, however, is the very definition of chaotic. Just diving right in and deciding that these gaps are thrilling and present an opportunity to learn and grow. Scientists have spent more time and money than I can calculate going as microscopic or telescopic as they can. They see the big picture in the most literal sense of the term, as well as every minute detail. An image of anything in the real world is available to us. We can see from the inside of an atom to a star billions of lightyears away. This is unbelievable, inconceivable, and beautiful. Pure chaos, and this is what we need to embrace. We have access to so much more potential than we allow ourselves to dream, and all we need to do to reach that potential is reach past the comfort of accepting the unknown as too far away to understand. Because it isn't.

I have one ask of you: Lean into the chaos. Dive headfirst into the world of the unknown that have been conditioned to be so scared of. We all would love to stay in our bubble of understanding. It is safe and comfortable and has no surprises to throw us off our game.

Meditation Activity

Here is a meditation exercise that you can try to expand your awareness and consciousness based on traditional visualization practices:

Find a quiet and comfortable place to sit where you won't be disturbed. Sit with your back straight and your feet on the ground. You can close your eyes or keep them open, whatever feels more comfortable for you.

Take a few deep breaths, inhaling through your nose and exhaling through your mouth. As you breathe, try to let go of any tension or stress in your body and mind.

Imagine that you are standing at the edge of a vast, open field. The sky is clear and bright blue, and there is a gentle breeze blowing. As you look out over the field, you can see a beautiful tree in the distance.

Begin to walk towards the tree. With each step, you feel more relaxed and at peace. You can feel the ground beneath your feet and the sun on your face.

As you approach the tree, you notice that there is a small door carved into the trunk. Open the door and step inside. The interior of the tree is warm and cozy, with soft light filtering through the leaves.

As you sit down and make yourself comfortable, take a moment to look around and notice the details of the space. You might see patterns in the wood, or small creatures moving around in the shadows.

Allow your awareness to expand beyond the boundaries of the tree. Imagine that you can see and feel everything that is happening in the field outside, and beyond that, in the surrounding landscape.

With each breath, feel your awareness expanding further and further, until you feel connected to everything around you. You might feel a sense of unity and oneness with the natural world.

When you are ready, slowly bring your awareness back to your physical body. Take a few deep breaths and wiggle your fingers and toes. Open your eyes if they are closed.

Take a moment to reflect on your experience. What did you notice during the meditation? How did you feel? You might want to journal your thoughts or simply take a few minutes to sit quietly and integrate the experience.

VII. CONCLUSION

The End... For Now

This book will probably be edited and re-released until I die. But for now I think we've got enough to be getting on with. Most of this quest for knowledge started when I asked myself one question:

What must I become to be who I am?

My journey thus far has led me to believe that integration is key. We must take the external realities of time, experiences and knowledge and marry them with our internal realities of values, desires and beliefs. The important revelation I had in all of this was that I have a choice. I have a choice to be who I am, to become who I want to be, and to be who I was born to become.

Life is an endless cycle of awakening, exploration, and integration. Start today, improve tomorrow, and who knows where you'll end up.

www.ingramcontent.com/pod-product-compliance
Lightning Source LLC
Chambersburg PA
CBHW070727130626
46553CB00005B/2176